The Bhagavad Gītā and the Bible: Pearls of the Same Strand

Edited and Compiled

by

Wade Hatcher

Published by

1992

Printed in the United States of America
ISBN 0-89716-415-6

Cover design: Wade Hatcher

Typesetting: Packard Productions

Published by
Peanut Butter Publishing
200 Second Avenue West
Seattle, WA 98119
(206) 281-5965

Contents

Editor's Preface

The original *Bhagavad Gītā*, a poem about eternity, is said to have been composed between 400 B.C. to 100 A.D. as an interpolation of the epic poem, the *Mahābhārata*. The *Gītā* relates the perceptions and wonders of God in a dialogue between Arjuna, the reluctant warrior disciple, and Krishna, the Godhead and Arjuna's spiritual guide. The setting of the dialogue is the great war in ancient India described in the *Mahābhārata*. Arjuna refuses to fight in the impending war set at the beginning of the *Gītā*. Krishna persuades Arjuna to go to battle in their ensuing dialogue, which forms the text of the *Gītā*. The presentation of concepts, such as selfless action while performing one's duty, the impossibility of death to the immortal indwelling Self, and the revelation of Krishna's divinity, omnipotence and omnipresence, help sway Arjuna's decision to go to battle. The wisdom woven into the *Bhagavad Gītā* extends the poem's scope far beyond Arjuna's initial predicament. The *Gītā* takes an unprejudiced view towards the multiplicity of seekers of Brahman/God and it presents an openhanded vision towards worship, which includes numerous pathways to God; as many pathways as there are seekers.

The *Bhagavad Gītā*, the essence of India's spiritual wisdom, has an enormous influence on Indian thought in particular and also to millions of truth seekers worldwide. The *Bible*, with unparalleled influence, is the guiding light to over one-fourth of the world's population. This book, titled *The Bhagavad Gītā and the Bible: Pearls of the Same Strand*, shows the similarity between the *Gītā* and the *Bible*. This book consists of excerpts from a larger study titled *The Bhagavad Gītā: With Parallel Passages From The Bible*, which matches around 620 of the 700 *Gītā* stanzas to similar *Bible* passages. This shortened work presents 180 *Gītā* stanzas with *Bible* passages. These two superficially different scriptures address the same topics of work, peace, divinity, immortality, devotion, renunciation, worship, desire, discrimination and impartiality.

In this condensed work, the corresponding parallels are arranged by chapter under different topical headings. The validity of the extracted parallels remains intact although they are removed from outside the original context of the complete *Bhagavad Gītā*. It is the editor's hope that this book will facilitate unity and understanding for readers of the *Gītā* and the *Bible*.

Wade Hatcher

Acknowledgments

Translations of the *Bhagavad Gītā* by Annie Besant, Jayadayal Goyandka, Raghavan Iyer, Juan Mascaro, Barbara Stoler Miller, Swami Vireswarananda, Winthrop Sargeant, Mahadeva Alladi Sastry, Swami Nikhilananda, Phulgenda Sinha, Swami Satchidananda and Bhaktivedanta Swami Prabhupāda have been consulted during the compilation of *The Bhagavad Gītā and the Bible: Pearls of the Same Strand*. The following *Bible* resources have contributed to this work; *Holy Bible: King James Version*, *The New International Version: New Testament*, *The Complete Bible: An American Translation*, *New World Translation of the Holy Scriptures*, *Cruden's Compact Concordance* and *Nave's Topical Bible*. I am thankful to all those above.

I am grateful to Teresa Nicota, who unknowingly was a motivating force behind this book. I am also appreciative to Lori Lively and Paul Franks for their helpful advice.

Work

In this path (way of action), Arjuna,
there is one thought of a resolute nature.
Many branched and endless
are the thoughts of the irresolute.

II:41

I am the way, the truth and the life.

John 14:6

Wisdom is before one who has understanding,
but the eyes of a fool are in the ends of the earth.

Proverbs 17:24

Steadfast in devotion, perform your works, Arjuna,
abandoning attachment,
be indifferent in success and failure.
Evenness is called yoga.

II:48

Therefore, my beloved brothers,
be steadfast, unmoveable,
always abounding in the work of the Lord,
because you know that your labor in the Lord
is not in vain.

I Corinthians 15:58

Love bears all things, believes all things,
hopes all things, endures all things.

I Corinthians 13:7

Whoever sees inaction in action,
and action in inaction,
they are yogis;
who have accomplished all action.

IV:18

My Father works up to this time,
and I work.

John 5:17

Perform your proper action,
for action is superior to inaction,
and even the maintenance of the body
is impossible for you without action.

III:8

Not slothful in work,
fervent in spirit,
serving the Lord.

Romans 12:11

Slothfulness casts one into a deep sleep,
and an idle soul shall suffer hunger.

Proverbs 19:15

This world is bound by action,
unless done for the purpose of sacrifice.
Perform sacrificial action, Arjuna,
free from attachment.

III:9

Except the Lord build the house,
they labor in vain who build it;
except the Lord keep the city,
the watchman keeps awake in vain.

Psalm 127:1

Let everything you do,
be done with charity.

I Corinthians 16:14

Therefore, without attachment,
constantly perform all dutiful action;
for truly, by performing action without attachment,
one reaches the Supreme.

III:19

The world passes away and the desire of it,
but whoso does the will of God abides forever.

I John 2:17

I have nothing to achieve in the three worlds, Arjuna,
nor is there anything unattained
that should be attained,
yet I engage in action.

III:22

There is one alone and not a second;
yes, he has neither child nor brother,
yet is there no end of all his labor,
nor is his eye satisfied with riches,
nor does he say, "For whom do I labor
and deprive my soul of good?"

Ecclesiastes 4:8

❖

Those who always practice this teaching of Mine,
full of faith and without finding fault,
are also freed from actions.

III:31

So I shall keep your law continually,
forever and ever.
I will walk at liberty,
for I seek your principles.

Psalm 119:44,45

Actions do not pollute Me,
nor do I desire the fruit of actions.
Whoso knows Me as such
is not bound by actions.

IV:14

Whoever has entered into his own rest
has also ceased from his own works,
just as God did from his.

Hebrew 4:10

Abandoning attachment to the fruit of action,
always content and dependent on none,
he does nothing at all,
even when engaged in action.

IV:20

Not that I speak of want,
for I have learned in whatever state I am,
to be content with that.
I can do everything through Christ,
which strengthens me.

Philippians 4:11,13

For one whose attachment is gone,
who is liberated
and established in knowledge;
his whole action melts away,
who acts for the sake of sacrifice.

IV:23

I came down from heaven,
not to do my own will,
but the will of him that sent me.

John 6:38

Truly, it is not possible
for embodied beings to abandon actions completely,
but he who abandons the fruit of actions
is said to be an abandoner.

XVIII:11

Man goes forth to his work,
and to his labor until the evening.

Psalm 104:23

The steps of a good person
are ordered by the Lord,
and he delights in his way.

Psalm 37:23

That action which is ordained,
free from attachment,
and done without desire or hatred,
by one who does not desire the fruit;
that action is declared to be enlightened.

XVIII:23

We are his workmanship,
created in Christ Jesus to do good works,
which God has ordained before
for us to walk in them.

Ephesians 2:10

Let the beauty of the Lord our God be upon us,
and you establish the work of our hands upon us.
Yea, the work of our hands, you establish it.

Psalm 90:17

The action which is performed
by one seeking to obtain desires,
with egotism or with great effort;
is said to be passionate.

XVIII:24

Whatever my eyes desired,
I did not keep from them.
I did not withhold my heart from any joy,
for my heart rejoiced in all my labor,
and this was my portion of all my labor.

Ecclesiastes 2:10

Whoso is greedy of gain
troubles their own house,

Proverbs 15:27

Even these actions (sacrifice, giving and austerity)
should be performed,
relinquishing attachment to the fruits;
this is My firm and highest belief, Arjuna.

XVIII:6

For do not let anyone think
that they will obtain anything from the Lord.

James 1:7

The action undertaken from delusion,
without regard to consequence,
loss or injury to others
or one's own capacity;
that is declared to be of darkness.

XVIII:25

He shuts his eyes to devise perverse things.

Proverbs 16:30

One should not give up the action
to which one is born, Arjuna,
for all undertakings are surrounded with defects,
as fire with smoke.

XVIII:48

Let everyone abide in the same calling
in which they were called.

I Corinthians 7:20

I have seen all the works
that are done under the sun,
and behold, all is vanity and vexation of spirit.
That which is crooked cannot be made straight,
and that which is lacking cannot be numbered.

Ecclesiastes 1:14,15

Some philosophers declare that action
should be abandoned as being evil,
while others declare that acts of sacrifice,
giving and austerity should not be given up.

XVIII:3

What profit does one have from all his labor,
which he does under the sun?

Ecclesiastes 1:3

Offer the sacrifices of righteousness,
and put your trust in the Lord.

Psalm 4:5

The steady-minded one, abandoning the fruit of action,
attains the peace born of devotion.
The unsteady one, attached to the fruit through desire,
is firmly bound.

V:12

The work of righteousness shall be peace;
the effect of righteousness;
quietness and assurance forever.

Isaiah 32:17

Everything is full of labor;
one cannot express it;
the eye is not satisfied with seeing,
nor the ear filled with hearing.

Ecclesiastes 1:8

Acts of sacrifice, giving and austerity
should be performed, not abandoned;
sacrifice, giving and austerity
are the purifiers of the wise.

XVIII:5

Those who have believed in God
should be careful to continue in good works.
These things are good and profitable to all.

Titus 3:8

Who gave himself for us,
that he may redeem us from all iniquity
and purify to himself his own people,
zealous of good works.

Titus 2:14

Discrimination

Those wise ones, endowed with understanding,
abandon the fruit of action,
and released from the bondage of rebirth,
they go to the place free of evil.

II:51

Do not store for yourselves treasures upon earth,
where moth and rust corrupts,
and where thieves break through and steal,
but store for yourselves treasures in heaven,
where moth nor rust corrupts,
and where thieves do not break through and steal.

Matthew 6:19,20

❖

When your mind transcends the mire of delusion,
then you will become disgusted
at what is yet to be heard
and what has been heard.

II:52

For we know in part and we prophesy in part,
but when the perfect comes,
then that which is in part shall be done away with.

I Corinthians 13:9,10

Whosoever rejoices only in the Self,
satisfied in the Self,
content only in the Self;
there is nothing for them to do.

III:17

As for me, I will behold
your face in righteousness;
I shall be satisfied,
when I awake with your likeness.

Psalm 17:16

❖

Even if you were the most evil
of all the sinners,
you shall truly cross over all sin
by the raft of wisdom.

IV:36

By mercy and truth, iniquity is purged.

Proverbs 16:6

Truly, there is no purifier
in this world equal to wisdom.
He who is perfected by yoga
finds this in time within the Self.

IV:38

Beloved, now we are the sons of God,
and it has not appeared what we will be.
Yet we know that when he appears,
we will be like him,
for we shall see him as he is.
Everyone who has this hope in him,
purifies themselves, even as he is pure.

I John 3:2,3

❖

Whoever is released
from these three gates of darkness, Arjuna,
does what is good for himself,
and thereby reaches the Supreme Goal.

XVI:22

I am the light of the world.
Whoso follows me shall not walk in darkness,
but shall have the light of life.

John 8:12

To those whose ignorance is destroyed
by the wisdom of the Self;
their wisdom, shining like the sun,
reveals the Supreme.

V:16

God, who commanded the light
to shine out of darkness,
has shined in our hearts,
to give the light of knowledge of God's glory
in the face of Jesus Christ.

II Corinthians 4:6

Whoever can endure here on earth,
before liberation from the body,
the impulse arising from desire and anger,
is disciplined and happy.

V:23

My brothers, count it all joy
when you fall into diverse temptations,
knowing that the testing of your faith
leads to patience.

James 1:2,3

Whenever the wavering and unsteady mind wanders away,
from there he should restrain it,
and bring it under control of the Self.

VI:26

*Casting down imaginations and every high thing
that exalts itself against the knowledge of God,
and bringing every thought into captivity
to the obedience of Christ.*

II Corinthians 10:5

Truly, My divine illusion,
made up of the material qualities,
is difficult to transcend.
Those who seek Me only
cross over this illusion.

VII:14

*Enter at the straight gate,
for wide is the gate and broad is the way
that leads to destruction,
and there are many who go through it.*

Matthew 7:13

*My eyes are always toward the Lord,
for he shall pluck my feet out of the net.*

Psalm 25:15

To you who does not find fault,
I shall declare this greatest secret;
knowledge combined with realization,
which having known, you shall be released from evil.

IX:1

Whoso listens to me shall dwell safely,
and be quiet from fear of evil.

Proverbs 1:33

The sovereign knowledge and secret,
the supreme purifier is this;
immediately comprehensible, unopposed to righteousness,
easy to perform and imperishable.

IX:2

For my yoke is easy and my burden is light.

Matthew 11:30

Righteousness shall go before him,
and shall set us in the way of his steps.

Psalm 85:13

The truth of the Lord endures forever.

Psalm 117:2

Whoever knows in truth
this glory and power of Mine,
is endowed with unshakeable Yoga;
there is no doubt about this.

X:7

*For yours is the kingdom,
the power and the glory forever.*

Matthew 6:13

❖

To those, who are always devoted to Me,
who worship Me with love,
I give the yoga of discrimination,
by which they come to Me.

X:10

*I will give them a heart to know me,
that I am the Lord.
They shall be my people,
and I will be their God,
for they shall return to me
with their whole heart.*

Jeremiah 24:7

From compassion for them,
I, dwelling in the Self,
destroy the darkness born of ignorance
with the shining lamp of wisdom.

X:11

*To the upright there arises light in the darkness.
He is gracious, full of compassion and righteous.*

Psalm 112:4

How shall I know You, Krishna,
always meditating on You?
In what aspects are You
to be thought of by me, Lord?

X:17

Let the words of my mouth
and the meditation of my heart
be acceptable in your sight, Lord,
my strength and redeemer.

Psalm 19:14

Constancy in knowledge of the Self,
seeing into the end of the knowledge of truth;
this is declared to be knowledge,
and its contrary is ignorance.

XIII:11

Seek the Lord and his strength,
seek his face continually.

I Chronicles 16:11

Now we see through a mirror, darkly,
but then face to face.
Now I know in part,
but then I shall know,
even as also I am known.

I Corinthians 13:12

The light even of lights,
that is said to be beyond darkness;
it is knowledge, the object of knowledge,
and by knowledge to be reached,
seated in the hearts of everyone.

XIII:17

This is the message we have heard from him
and declare to you, "That God is light,
and there is no darkness in him at all."

I John 1:5

God, who commanded the light
to shine out of darkness,
has shined in our hearts
to give the light of the knowledge
of God's glory in the face of Jesus Christ.

II Corinthians 4:6

❖

The deluded do not perceive Him,
who departs, stays,
or enjoys nature's material qualities;
they see, who possess the eye of knowledge.

XV:10

The material man does not receive
the things of the Spirit of God,
for they are foolishness to him,
nor can he know them,
because they are spiritually discerned.

I Corinthians 2:14

Those striving yogis
perceive Him dwelling in the Self,
but though striving, those of untrained self,
the unintelligent, do not perceive Him.

XV:11

It is the Spirit of truth,
which the world cannot receive,
because it does not see him nor knows him.
You know him, for he dwells with you
and is within you.

John 14:17

❖

The scripture is your authority
in deciding what should be done
and what is not to be done.
Knowing what has been declared by scriptural ordinance,
perform your duty in this world.

XVI:24

All scripture is given by inspiration of God,
and is useful for doctrine, rebuke,
correction and instruction in righteousness,

II Timothy 3:16

That understanding which enveloped in ignorance,
seeing wrong to be right,
and everything in perverse ways,
is of darkness, Arjuna.

XVIII:32

*Woe to them that call evil good and good evil;
that put darkness for light and light for darkness;
that put bitter for sweet and sweet for bitter!*

Isaiah 5:20

Resigning all actions to Me in thought,
regarding Me as the supreme,
resorting to the yoga of discrimination,
think of Me always.

XVIII:57

*Whatever you do, do it with all your heart
for the Lord and not to people,*

Colossians 3:23

*Give me your heart,
and let your eyes observe my ways.*

Proverbs 23:26

My delusion is destroyed
and I have gained wisdom through Your grace, Krishna.
I stand without doubt
and will do Your word.

XVIII:73

I have chosen the way of truth;
your judgments I have laid before me.

Psalm 119:30

❖

They are all noble,
but the wise man, I think to be truly My Self,
for steadfast in mind,
he resorts to Me as the highest goal.

VII:18

Blessed is the one who hears me,
watching daily at my gates;
waiting at the posts of my doors.

Proverbs 8:34

That by which one sees
one indestructible being in all beings,
undivided among the divided;
know that knowledge to be enlightened.

XVIII:20

So we, being many,
are one body in Christ,
and everyone are members,
one of another.

Romans 12:5

That which sees separation
in diverse beings of various kinds
among all beings;
know that knowledge to be passionate.

XVIII:21

You are still worldly.
Since there is envying, strife
and divisions among you,
are you not worldly and walk as men?

I Corinthians 3:3

❖

That which clings to one thing
as if it were all,
devoid of reason,
and unconcerned for reality, and narrow,
is said to be of darkness.

XVIII:22

The lazy one is wiser in his own conceit
than seven people who can give a reason.

Proverbs 26:16

You are unable to see Me
with these eyes of yours.
I give you a divine eye;
behold My majestic Yoga.

XI:8

Now we have not received the spirit of the world,
but the spirit which comes from God,
that we may know the things
God has freely given us.

I Corinthians 2:12

Devotion

They, who know Me in the perishable existence,
in the spirit and in sacrifice,
know Me even at the time of death,
steadfast in mind.

VII:30

*So also now, Christ shall be exalted in my body,
whether it be by life or death.*

Philippians 1:20

To the ever devoted yogi,
who constantly thinks of Me
with an undivided mind,
I am easily reached, Arjuna.

VIII:14

*We become partners of Christ,
if we hold the beginning of our confidence
steadfast until the end.*

Hebrews 3:14

Always glorifying Me,
striving with firm vows, and reverent,
they worship Me with devotion,
always steadfast.

IX:14

*Lord, I have loved the dwelling of your house,
and the place where your honor dwells.
My foot stands in an even place;
in the congregations I will bless the Lord.*

Psalm 26:8,12

❖

Even if the most evil worships Me
with exclusive devotion,
he is considered righteous,
for he is rightly resolved.

IX:30

*If anyone is in Christ,
he is a new being;
old things have passed away,
and behold, everything becomes new.*

II Corinthians 5:17

Keep your mind on Me, be devoted to Me,
sacrifice and bow down to Me.
Thus steadfast, with Me as your supreme goal,
you shall come to Me.

IX:34

From now on, if you shall seek the Lord your God,
you shall find him,
if you seek him with all your heart
and with all your soul.

Deuteronomy 4:29

By undistracted devotion alone
can I be known of this form,
and be seen in truth,
and entered into, Arjuna.

XI:54

As it is written,
eye has not seen, nor ear heard,
nor has it entered into the heart of man,
the things which God has prepared
for those who love him.

I Corinthians 2:9

To those who worship Me alone,
thinking of no other;
to them who are always steadfast,
I secure gain and safety.

IX:22

First seek the kingdom of God,
and his righteousness,
and all these things shall be added to you.

Matthew 6:33

Those who worship Me,
renouncing all actions in Me,
regarding Me as Supreme,
meditating on Me with exclusive devotion;
for those whose thought is focused on Me,
I am soon, Arjuna,
the deliverer from the ocean of death and rebirth.

XII:6,7

Because he has set his love upon me,
I will deliver him.
I will set him on high
because he has known my name.

Psalm 91:14

Truly, those who follow this immortal law as taught here,
who are endowed with faith, and devoted,
and look at Me as the Supreme;
they are very dear to Me.

XII:20

Whoever has and keeps my commandments, loves me.
Whoever loves me, shall be loved by my Father,
and I will love and show myself to them.

John 14:21

Unwavering devotion to Me
through the yoga of non-separation,
retreating to solitary places,
aversion to worldly society.

XIII:10

*Whom have I in heaven but you?
And there is nothing upon earth
that I desire beside you.*

Psalm 73:25

*My people shall dwell in a peaceful habitation,
sure dwellings and quiet resting places.*

Isaiah 32:18

*Do not be unequally yoked
together with unbelievers,
for what fellowship does righteousness have
with unrighteousness?
Or what communion does light have
with darkness?*

II Corinthians 6:14

❖

Yet others, ignorant of the Self,
worship by hearing from others,
and they also transcend death,
devoted to what they heard.

XIII:25

*It is written in the prophets,
"They shall all be taught of God."
Therefore everyone who has heard
and learned of the Father, comes to me.
Truly, I say, "one who believes in me
has everlasting life."*

John 6:45,47

Whoever serves Me
with the unwavering yoga of devotion,
transcending nature's three qualities,
is ready to become like God.

XIV:26

Truly, my soul waits upon God;
from him comes my salvation.

Psalm 62:1

All of us with unveiled faces,
reflecting like mirrors
the glory of the Lord,
are changed into the same image
with great glory,
even by the spirit of the Lord.

II Corinthians 3:18

The faith of each is in accordance
with his nature, Arjuna.
People are made up of their faith;
as a person's faith is, so is he.

XVII:3

According to your faith,
be it unto you.

Matthew 9:29

Focus your mind on Me, be devoted to Me,
worship Me, bow down to Me;
you shall reach Myself, I promise,
for you are dear to Me.

XVIII:65

You shall seek and find me
when you shall search for me
with all your heart.

Jeremiah 29:13

❖

This is not to be spoken (devotion to Krishna)
to one without austerity nor devotion,
nor to one who does not desire to listen,
nor to one who speaks evil of Me.

XVIII:67

Do not give what is holy to the dogs,
nor cast your pearls before swine,
for they may trample them under their feet,
and turn again and tear up you.

Matthew 7:6

❖

Whoever will declare this supreme secret
among my worshippers,
having shown the highest devotion to Me,
shall doubtlessly come to Me.

XVIII:68

What we have seen and heard, we declare to you,
so that you also may have fellowship with us,
for our fellowship is with the Father
and with his Son, Jesus Christ.

I John 1:3

Always keeping the self steadfast,
freed from sins,
the yogi easily attains
the infinite joy of contact with God.

VI:28

For our heart shall rejoice in him,
because we have trusted in his holy name.

Psalm 33:21

To him that is able to keep you from falling,
and that can present you as faultless
in the presence of his glory with exceeding joy,

Jude 24

How much easier it is (to reach the Supreme goal)
for holy priests and devoted royal saints!
Reaching this transient and joyless world,
devote yourself to Me.

IX:33

God, you are my God.
I will seek you early;
my soul thirsts for you.
My flesh longs for you
in a dry and thirsty land
where no water is.

Psalm 63:1

Renunciation

When a person abandons all desires of the mind,
satisfied in the Self by oneself,
then one is said to be steady in knowledge.

II:55

A good person shall be satisfied from oneself.

Proverbs 14:14

❖

When he completely withdraws the senses
from the objects of the senses,
as the tortoise does its limbs,
his knowledge is steady.

II:58

While we do not look at the things which are seen,
but at what is unseen,
for the things seen are temporal,
but what is unseen is eternal.

II Corinthians 4:18

Sense-objects fade away from the fasting embodied one,
but not the taste.
On seeing the Supreme,
his taste ceases also.

II:59

Looking with diligence,
so not to miss the grace of God,
so no root of bitterness
springs up to trouble you,
and by which many are defiled;

Hebrews 12:15

The kingdom of heaven is like a treasure
buried in a field,
which a man found and hid again.
Then from his joy,
he sold everything and bought that field.

Matthew 13:44

Freed from passion, fear and anger,
absorbed in Me, taking refuge in Me,
purified by the austerity of wisdom,
many have reached My being.

IV:10

Blessed are the pure in heart,
for they shall see God.

Matthew 5:8

The sages attain absorption in God,
whose sins have been destroyed,
and doubts have been removed,
who are self-controlled,
and intent on the welfare of all beings.

V:25

Whoever is born of God does not sin,
for their seed remains in him;
they cannot sin because they are born of God.
Whoever does not do what is right is not of God,
nor are they who do not love their brother.

I John 3:9,10

Know yoga, Arjuna,
to be what they call renunciation;
indeed, no one becomes a yogi,
who has not renounced self-interest.

VI:2

Set your affection on things above,
not on things on the earth.
For you are dead,
and your life is hid with Christ in God.

Colossians 3:2,3

When he is not attached to sense objects
or to actions,
renouncing all self-interest,
then he is said to have attained Yoga.

VI:4

What things were gain to me,
those I counted loss for Christ.

Philippians 3:7

Abandoning without exception
all desires born of the will,
and completely restraining the senses
from all sides with the mind.

VI:24

Teaching us that
denying ungodliness and worldly desires,
we should live soberly, righteously and godly
in this present world;

Titus 2:12

Indifferent, pure, capable,
disinterested, untroubled,
renouncing all undertakings and devoted to Me,
one is dear to Me.

XII:16

Yea, doubtlessly, I count everything a loss
compared with the excellency of the knowledge
of Christ Jesus my Lord,
for whose sake I have lost everything,
and do count it as rubbish,
so that I may win Christ.

Philippians 3:8

❖

Dispassion for sense objects,
absence of egotism;
insight into the evil of birth,
death, old age, sickness and pain;

XIII:8

Do not love the world,
nor the things that are in the world.
If anyone loves the world,
the love of the Father is not in him.

I John 2:15

Before honor is humility.

Proverbs 15:33

The person is likened to vanity;
his days are as a shadow that passes away.

Psalm 144:4

For we know that the whole creation groans
and toils in pain together until now.

Romans 8:22

One neither hates
light, activity or delusion when present,
nor desires them when absent, Arjuna.

XIV:22

Not that I speak of want,
for I have learned
in whatever state I am in,
to be content with that.

Philippians 4:11

Free from pride and delusion,
with the evil of attachment conquered,
always dwelling in the Self,
rid of desires,
released from the dualities
known as pleasure and pain,
the undeluded reach the Eternal goal.

XV:5

Stand fast in the liberty
by which Christ has made us free,
and do not be entangled again
with the yoke of bondage.

Galatians 5:1

Dwelling in solitude, eating but little,
subduing speech, body and mind,
always engaged in the yoga of meditation,
cultivating dispassion.

XVIII:52

I am like a pelican of the wilderness.
I am like an owl of the desert.
I watch and am like a sparrow
alone upon the housetop.

Psalm 102:6,7

Let your moderation be known to all.

Philippians 4:5

My soul waits for the Lord
more that they who watch for the morning,
I say, more than they who watch for the morning.

Psalm 130:6

Better is a dry morsel,
and quietness with that,
than a house full of sacrifices with strife.

Proverbs 17:1

The yogi should constantly steady the mind,
remaining in solitude,
alone, with the mind and body controlled,
free from desire and possessions.

VI:10

He sits alone and keeps silence,
because he has borne it upon himself.

Lamentations 3:28

And having food and clothing,
let us be content with that.

I Timothy 6:8

Abandoning egotism, force, pride,
desire, anger, possessiveness,
selfless and peaceful,
one is fit to be one with God.

XVIII:53

Whoever will save his life shall lose it,
and whoever will lose his life for my sake
shall find it.

Matthew 16:25

Let this mind be in you,
which was also in Christ Jesus,
who being in the form of God,
did not think it robbery
to be equal with God,

Philippians 2:5,6

Free from desire,
with the mind and the self controlled,
relinquishing all possessions,
and doing bodily action only,
one incurs no evil.

IV:21

If anyone will come after me,
let them deny themselves,
and take up their cross daily and follow me.

Luke 9:23

The foxes have holes
and the birds of the air have nests,
but the Son of man has no place
to lay his head.

Matthew 8:20

Whosoever is dead is free from sin.

Romans 6:7

Worship

With my heart overcome by the weakness of self-pity;
my mind confused as to my duty,
I ask you, what is absolutely good.
I am your disciple.
Tell me, who pleads of you.

II:7

From the end of the earth I will cry to you
when my heart is overwhelmed;
lead me to the rock that is higher than I.

Psalm 61:2

By whatever way they approach Me,
so I do reward them;
people follow My path in every way, Arjuna.

IV:11

A person's work he shall render to him,
and cause everyone to find according to his way.

Job 34:11

A person's heart devises his way
but the Lord directs the steps.

Proverbs 16:9

Some yogis offer sacrifices to the gods;
others offer themselves as a sacrifice
in the fire of God.

IV:25

To love him with all the heart,
with all the understanding,
with all the soul and with all the strength,
and to love his neighbor as himself,
is more than all whole burnt offerings
and sacrifices.

Mark 12:33

❖

That yogi, who established in oneness,
and who worships Me as abiding in all beings,
lives in Me, whatever one's way of life.

VI:31

To us there is only one God, the Father,
from whom everything comes, and in whom we live;
and there is one Lord Jesus Christ,
by whom all things come and by whom we live.

I Corinthians 8:6

A yogi, who strives with diligence,
purified from sin,
and perfected through many births,
then reaches the supreme goal.

VI:45

Blessed are those who hunger
and thirst after righteousness,
for they shall be filled.
Blessed are the pure in heart,
for they shall see God.

Matthew 5:6,8

❖

Among thousands of people,
one perhaps strives for perfection;
even among those who strive,
and with those who are perfected,
only one perhaps knows Me in truth.

VII:3

Straight is the gate
and narrow is the way,
which leads to life,
and there are few who find it.

Matthew 7:14

Whatever sacrifice or gift is made
and whatever austerity is practiced,
which is without faith, is called *asat*, Arjuna;
it is nothing here or after death.

XVII:28

Without faith it is impossible to please God,
for whoso comes to God must believe that he is,
and that he is a rewarder
of those who diligently seek him.

Hebrews 11:6

❖

Worshipping through the sacrifice of knowledge,
others worship Me as the one and the manifold,
in various manifestations, everywhere present.

IX:15

The manifestation of the Spirit
is given to each one
to benefit from that.

I Corinthians 12:7

Even those who worship other gods,
endowed with faith,
also worship Me, Arjuna,
though contrary to rules.

IX:23

You shall have no other gods before me.

Exodus 20:3

Whatever you do, eat, sacrifice, give,
and in whatever austerities you perform;
do it as an offering to Me.

IX:27

Therefore, whether you eat, drink,
or whatever you do;
do all for the glory of God.

I Corinthians 10:31

❖

Therefore, bowing down, prostrating my body,
I ask You, adorable Lord, to forgive.
As father with son, as friend with friend,
as lover to beloved, bear with me.

XI:44

There is forgiveness with you,
that you may be revered.

Psalm 130:4

❖

Greater is their difficulty,
whose thoughts are fixed on the Unmanifest,
for the goal of the Unmanifest
is difficult for the embodied to reach.

XII:5

That which is far off and exceedingly deep,
who can find it out?

Ecclesiastes 7:24

Those of pure actions,
whose sin has come to an end,
who are freed from the delusion of duality,
worship Me with firm resolve.

VII:28

Now the end of the commandment
is love out of a pure heart,
a good conscience and genuine faith.

I Timothy 1:5

❖

That sacrifice is of light,
which is offered by those desiring no reward,
in observation of the scriptures,
with a firm resolve in the mind
that they should merely sacrifice.

XVII:11

Jesus said, "My food is to do the will
of him that sent me,
and to finish his work."

John 4:34

Oh, that my ways were directed
to keep your statutes!

Psalm 119:5

The sacrifice which is offered
with a view for reward and ostentation;
know that to be of passion, Arjuna.

XVII:12

They sacrifice into their net,
and burn incense into their drag,
because by themselves their portion is fat
and their meat plenteous.

Habakkuk 1:16

All their works are done
to be seen by others.

Matthew 23:5

The sacrifice which is contrary to scriptures,
in which no food is offered,
without chants and gifts, and empty of faith,
is said to be of darkness.

XVII:13

The sacrifice of the wicked
is an abomination to the Lord;

Proverbs 15:8

The great souls, Arjuna,
worship Me with mind turned to no other,
abiding in the divine nature,
knowing Me as the imperishable source of beings.

IX:13

*There is no one holy as the Lord,
for there is no one beside you.*

I Samuel 2:2

*You, Lord, remain forever.
Your throne is from generation to generation.*

Lamentations 5:19

Now hear from Me, Arjuna,
of the three kinds of happiness,
one of which is enjoyed through practice
and brings an end to pain.

XVIII:36

*Let all those that seek you,
rejoice and be glad in you.*

Psalm 40:16

*God shall wipe away all tears from their eyes,
and there shall be no more death, sorrow, crying,
nor shall there be any more pain,
for the former things have passed away.*

Revelation 21:4

Peace

In peace all sorrows end,
for the reason of the tranquil-minded
soon becomes steady.

II:65

*Peace I leave with you, my peace I give to you;
not as the world gives, do I give to you.
Do not let your heart be troubled,
nor let it be afraid.*

John 14:27

*The peace of God,
which passes all understanding,
shall keep your hearts and minds
through Christ Jesus.*

Philippians 4:7

When all desires enter,
like waters enter the ocean,
which becomes filled yet remains unaltered,
he attains peace; not one who desires objects.

II:70

*Better is a handful with quietness,
than both hands full with trouble
and vexation of spirit.*

Ecclesiastes 4:6

The person finds peace,
who abandons all desires,
acting without attachment,
possessiveness or egotism.

II:71

Come to me, all of you who labor
and are heavily burdened,
and I will give you rest.
Take my yoke upon you and learn of me,
for I am meek and humble in heart,
and you shall find rest for your souls.

Matthew 11:28,29

Anyone attains wisdom who is faithful,
devoted to that, and with subdued senses.
Having attained wisdom,
soon they reach the supreme peace.

IV:39

Happy is the one who finds wisdom,
and one who gains understanding.
Her ways are those of satisfaction,
and all her paths are peace.

Proverbs 3:13,17

Always disciplining the mind,
the yogi whose mind is subdued
attains the peace,
the supreme bliss abiding within Me.

VI:15

You will keep him in perfect peace,
whose mind remains on you,
because he trusts in you.

Isaiah 26:3

❖

As a lamp in a windless spot does not waver,
so there is the simile
of the yogi of subdued thought,
absorbed in the yoga of the Self.

VI:19

A person will be like a hiding place
from the wind,
and a shelter from the tempest;

Isaiah 32:2

One should withdraw little by little,
with intelligence held in firmness.
Establishing the mind in the Self,
he should not think of anything.

VI:25

Be still, and know that I am God.

Psalm 46:10

Knowledge is indeed better than practice;
meditation is better than knowledge;
abandonment of the fruits of action
is better than meditation;
from abandonment peace soon follows.

XII:12

Lord, you will ordain peace for us,
for you also have performed all our works in us.

Isaiah 26:12

Knowing Me, the enjoyer of sacrifices and austerities,
the mighty Lord of all the worlds,
and the friend of all beings,
one attains peace.

V:29

Now acquaint yourself with him,
and be at peace;
by this good shall come to you.

Job 22:21

IMPARTIALITY

The omnipresent Lord does not take the evil
or the good deed of anyone.
Wisdom is enveloped by ignorance;
because of this, people are deluded.

V:15

If you sin, what do you do against him?
If your transgressions are multiplied,
what do you do to him?
If you are righteous, what do you give him,
or what does he receive from your hand?

Job 35:6,7

Seeing many things, but you do not observe;
opening the ears, but you do not hear.

Isaiah 42:20

A person excels, who is impartial
to the good-hearted, friends and enemies,
the indifferent, the neutral and adversaries,
kinsmen, the righteous and the unrighteous.

VI:9

These things also belong to the wise.
It is not good to have respect
of persons in judgment.

Proverbs 24:23

The self, steadfast in yoga,
sees the same everywhere,
with the Self abiding in all beings,
and all beings in the Self.

VI:29

There is neither Jew nor Greek,
slave nor free, male nor female,
for you are all one in Christ Jesus.

Galatians 3:28

❖

At the end of many births,
the person of wisdom comes to Me,
realizing that Krishna is all;
such a noble soul is very difficult to find.

VII:19

Having put on the new self,
renewed in knowledge
after the image of God that created him,
where there is neither Greek nor Jew,
circumcision nor uncircumcision,
barbarian, Scythian, slave nor free,
but Christ is all, and in all.

Colossians 3:10,11

I am the same to all beings;
there is none hated or dear to Me,
but they who worship Me with devotion
are in Me, and I am also in them.

IX:29

There is no respect of persons with God.

Romans 2:11

If anyone loves me,
they will keep my words.
My Father will love them,
and we will come and abide with them.

John 14:23

Non-attachment, absence of self-identification
to son, wife, home and the like,
and constant equanimity toward
desirable and undesirable events.

XIII:9

If anyone comes to me
and does not hate his father,
mother, wife, children, brothers,
sisters and their own lives also,
they cannot be my disciple.

Luke 14:26

Godliness with contentment is great gain.

I Timothy 6:6

The wise see the same
in a priest endowed with wisdom and humility,
in a cow and an elephant,
as also in a dog and one who eats dogs.

V:18

We walk by faith, not by sight.
We are confident and would prefer
to be absent from the body
and to be present with the Lord.

II Corinthians 5:7,8

DESIRE

The contacts with matter
cause heat and cold, pleasure and pain;
they come and go and are impermanent.
Endure them bravely, Arjuna.

II:14

Do not love the world,
nor the things that are in the world.
If anyone loves the world,
the love of the Father is not in them.
The world passes away and the desire of it,

I John 2:15,17

By dwelling on the sense objects,
attachment for them arises;
from attachment arises desire;
from desire arises anger;

II:62

Everyone is tempted,
when drawn away by their own desire and enticed.

James 1:14

From where come the wars
and fighting among you?
Do they not come from your own lusts
that battle within you?

James 4:1

To the unsteady there is neither wisdom,
nor meditation;
to the unmeditative there is no peace,
and without peace how can there be happiness?

II:66

Better is the sight of the eyes
than the wandering of desire;
this is also vanity and vexation of spirit.

Ecclesiastes 6:9

❖

Attraction and hatred are rooted
in the object of each sense;
one should not come under the sway of these two,
for they are his enemies.

III:34

You adulterous people, do you not know
that friendship with the world
is enmity with God?
Therefore, whoever is a friend of the world
is the enemy of God.

James 4:4

Dragged on by what,
does one commit sin,
even though reluctantly, Krishna,
as if constrained by force?

III:36

The good that I want to do,
I do not,
but the evil which I do not want,
that I do.

Romans 7:19

This is desire and anger,
born of passion,
all devouring and greatly sinful;
know this to be the enemy here.

III:37

Then after desire has conceived,
it brings forth sin;
and sin, when it is finished,
brings forth death.

James 1:15

❖

As fire is surrounded by smoke,
as a mirror by dust,
and as the embryo is enclosed in the womb,
so is wisdom covered by desire.

III:38

From where then does wisdom come,
and where is the place of understanding?
It is hidden from the eyes of all the living,
and kept concealed from the birds of the air.

Job 28:20,21

Through desire, a person having separated oneself,
seeks and interferes with all wisdom.

Proverbs 18:1

Those delights born of external contacts
are truly sources of pain,
for they have a beginning and ending, Arjuna;
the wise person does not rejoice in them.

V:22

There is a way which seems right to a person,
but the end of it are the ways of death.
Even in laughter the heart is sorrowful,
and the end of that joy is heaviness.

Proverbs 14:12,13

With their wisdom led away by desire,
they resort to other gods,
practicing various religious rites,
limited by their own nature.

VII:20

You know you were idolaters,
carried away by dumb idols,
just as you were led.

I Corinthians 12:2

Know passion to be emotional,
the source of thirst and attachment;
it binds down the embodied self, Arjuna,
by attachment to action.

XIV:7

All things are full of labor;
one cannot express it;
the eye is not satisfied with seeing,
nor the ear filled from hearing.

Ecclesiastes 1:8

Bound by a hundred ties of hope,
given over to lust and anger,
they seek hoards of wealth by unjust ways
to gratify their desires.

XVI:12

*Your riches are corrupted,
and your garments are motheaten.
You have lived on earth
in pleasure and self-indulgence.
You have fattened your hearts
like in a day of slaughter.*

James 5:2,5

❖

This has been gained by me today,
and this desire I shall attain;
this is mine,
and this wealth shall also be mine.

XVI:13

*You say in your heart,
my power and the strength of my hand
has gained for me this wealth.*

Deuteronomy 8:17

Bewildered by many thoughts,
entangled in the snare of delusion,
addicted to the gratification of lust,
they fall into a foul hell.

XVI:16

*Those who want to be rich
fall into temptation, a trap
and into many foolish and hurtful lusts,
which drown men in destruction and ruin.*

I Timothy 6:9

There are three gates of hell,
destructive of the self:
lust, anger and greed.
Therefore one should renounce these three.

XVI:21

I urge you as strangers and pilgrims,
abstain from fleshly lusts,
which war against the soul.

I Peter 2:11

Cease from anger and forsake wrath;
do not worry in anyway to do evil.
For evildoers shall be cut off;

Psalm 37:8,9

Do not labor to be rich.

Proverbs 23:4

Whoso acts under the impulse of desire,
casting aside the ordinance of scriptures,
does not attain perfection,
nor happiness, nor the Supreme Goal.

XVI:23

For you may know,
that no immoral, impure, covetous person,
who is an idolater,
has any inheritance in the kingdom
of Christ and God.

Ephesians 5:5

They say, "the universe is without truth
or basis, without a God,
born of mutual union,
brought about by lust, how else?"

XVI:8

The fool has said in his heart,
there is no God.
They are corrupt and have done abominable works.
There is no one that does good.

Psalm 14:1

Therefore God also abandoned them to impurity
through the lusts of their own hearts
to dishonor their own bodies between themselves.
They changed the truth of God into a lie,
and worshipped and served the created
more than the Creator, who is blessed forever.

Romans 1:24,25

Obsessed with immeasurable cares,
ending only with death,
regarding gratification of desire
as their highest aim,
assured that this is all.

XVI:11

You who dwell upon many waters,
abundant in treasures,
your end has come,
and the measure of your covetousness.

Jeremiah 51:13

By the delusion of opposite dualities,
arising from desire and aversion,
all beings are deluded at birth, Arjuna.

VII:27

Yet man is born into trouble,
as sparks fly upward.

Job 5:7

❖

I am rich and well born.
Who else is equal to me?
I will sacrifice, give and rejoice—
thus deluded by ignorance.

XVI:15

The rich man's wealth is his strong city,
and like a high wall in his own conceit.

Proverbs 18:11

Divine Manifestations

One sees the Self as a wonder,
another speaks of the Self as a wonder,
and another hears of the Self as a wonder,
yet on hearing of it, no one understands the Self.

II:29

Great is the Lord and greatly to be praised;
his greatness is unsearchable.

Psalm 145:3

Although I am birthless, imperishable,
and Lord of all beings,
yet ruling over My own material nature,
I am born by My own wondrous power.

IV:6

In the beginning was the Word,
and the Word was God.
Everything was made by him,
and apart from him nothing has been made.
The Word became flesh and lived among us,
and we saw his glory,
of the only born of the Father,
full of grace and truth.

John 1:1,3,14

The foolish ones regard Me, the unmanifest,
as coming into manifestation,
not knowing My higher, imperishable,
unsurpassed nature.

VII:24

You know me and you know where I am from,
and I have not come here on my own,
but he that sent me is real,
whom you do not know.

John 7:28

He that descended is also the same one
that ascended up far above all heavens,
so he may fill everything.

Ephesians 4:10

I am not manifest to all,
veiled by My mysterious power.
This deluded world does not know Me,
unborn and imperishable.

VII:25

In him was life,
and that life was the light of all.
The light shined in darkness,
and the darkness did not comprehend it.

John 1:4,5

At the coming of day
the manifest proceeds from the unmanifest;
at the coming of night
all is dissolved in the unmanifest again.

VIII:18

In the beginning God created the heaven and earth.
The earth was without form, and void,
and darkness was upon the face of the deep.
The spirit of God moved
upon the face of the waters.

Genesis 1:1,2

The day of the Lord will come
like a thief in the night,
in which the heavens shall pass away
with a great noise,
and the elements shall melt with intense heat.
Also the earth and the works therein
shall be burned up.

II Peter 3:10

The foolish disregard Me,
who have taken a human form,
not knowing My higher nature
as the great Lord of beings.

IX:11

Who is a liar, if it is not he,
who denies that Jesus is the Christ?
He is anti-christ,
who denies the Father and Son.

I John 2:22

You know Yourself through the Self,
Supreme Spirit, Source of beings,
Lord of beings, God of gods,
Ruler of the world.

X:15

I and my Father are one.

John 10:30

I shall tell you
of My chief heavenly glories, Arjuna,
for there is no limit to My extent.

X:19

His work is honorable and glorious,
and his righteousness endures forever.

Psalm 111:3

Who does great things past finding out,
and wonders without number.

Job 9:10

I am also the seed of all beings, Arjuna;
there is no being, animate or inanimate,
that can exist without Me.

X:39

God gives it a body as he pleases
and to every seed its own body.

I Corinthians 15:38

He gives to all life, breath and everything.

Acts 17:25

There is no end of My heavenly glories, Arjuna.
What I have described are mere examples
of the extent of My powers.

X:40

Which does great and unsearchable things;
wonders without number;

Job 5:9

Behold, these are parts of his ways,
but how little a portion is heard of him?

Job 26:14

❖

Whatever being is glorious,
beautiful and powerful,
understand that to be
a fragment of My splendor.

X:41

To everyone of us is given grace
according to the measure of the gift of Christ.

Ephesians 4:7

❖

Whatever was rashly said by me
through carelessness or affection,
addressing You as, "Krishna, cousin, friend",
thinking of You as merely a friend,
ignorant of Your greatness—
if in jest, I insulted You at play,
at rest, while sitting or eating,
when alone or in the presence of others, O Immortal One,
I ask forgiveness of You, Boundless One.

XI:41,42

The son of man has come eating and drinking,
and you say, "Behold a glutton,
a drinker, a friend of tax-collectors and sinners."

Luke 7:34

This (world) is My lower nature,
but distinct from this is My higher nature,
in the form of indwelling souls, Arjuna,
which uphold this universe.

VII:5

*The first self is of the earth, earthy;
the second self is the Lord from heaven.*

I Corinthians 15:47

Spectator, permitter,
supporter, enjoyer, the Great Lord,
the Supreme Self
and the Supreme Spirit in this body.

XIII:22

*His eyes are upon the ways of people,
and he sees all their steps.*

Job 34:21

*The Lord has made everything for himself,
yea, even the wicked for the day of evil.*

Proverbs 16:4

*Even to your old age I am he;
to gray hairs I will carry you.
I have made, and I will bear,
I will carry, and I will deliver you.*

Isaiah 46:4

*You have created everything,
and for your pleasure
they exist and were created.*

Revelation 4:11

Great is our Lord and of great power;

Psalm 147:5

*By this we know that we dwell in him,
and he in us,
because he has given us of his Spirit.*

I John 4:13

One sees, who sees all actions
performed by material nature alone,
and the Self not acting.

XIII:29

Your way is in the sea,
your path in the great waters,
and your footsteps are not known.

Psalm 77:19

❖

As the one sun illumines the whole world,
so does the embodied Self
illumine all bodies, Arjuna.

XIII:33

In him was life,
and the life was the light of all.
That was the true Light,
which lights everyone
who comes into the world.

John 1:4,9

The great God is my womb;
in that I place the seed;
from that is the origin of all beings.

XIV:3

Did not he that made me in the womb, make them?
Did not one fashion us in the womb?

Job 31:15

Have we not all one Father?
Has not one God created us?

Malachi 2:10

Presiding over the ears,
the eyes, the senses of touch,
taste, smell and also the mind,
He enjoys the sense objects.

XV:9

Does he that planted the ear, not hear?
Does he that formed the eye, not see?

Psalm 94:9

Omnipresence

Those who see Me everywhere,
and see everything in Me;
I am not lost to them,
nor are they lost to Me.

VI:30

Where shall I go from your spirit?
Where shall I flee from your presence?
If I ascend into heaven, you are there.
If I make my bed in hell, behold, you are there.

Psalm 139:7,8

There is nothing higher than I, Arjuna.
All this is strung on Me
as clusters of pearls on a strand.

VII:7

One God and Father of all,
who is above all,
through all and in you all.

Ephesians 4:6

I am the source of all.
Everything evolves from Me.
Thinking this, the wise worship Me,
endowed with contemplation.

X:8

Of him, through him and to him, are all things;
to whom be glory forever.

Romans 11:36

I am the Self, Arjuna,
seated in the heart of all beings;
I am the beginning, middle
and end of all beings.

X:20

On that day you shall know
that I am in my Father,
you in me and I in you.

John 14:20

I am the Alpha and Omega,
the beginning and the end,
the first and the last.

Revelation 22:13

Arjuna saw the whole universe
established in one,
with many divisions
in the body of the God of gods.

XI:13

So we, being many,
are one body in Christ,
and everyone members, one of another.

Romans 12:5

This space between heaven and earth,
and all directions are filled by You alone.
Seeing this, Your marvelous and terrible form,
the three worlds tremble, O mighty Lord.

XI:20

"Do I not fill heaven and earth,"
said the Lord?

Jeremiah 23:24

You mountains, that skipped like rams,
and you little hills, like lambs?
Tremble earth, at the presence of the Lord,

Psalm 114:6,7

With hands, feet, eyes,
heads, faces and hearing everywhere,
it exists, enveloping all.

XIII:13

He is before everything,
and by him everything exists.

Colossians 1:17

IMMORTALITY

I never did not exist,
nor you, nor these rulers of people;
nor shall we ever cease to exist hereafter.

II:12

*So when this perishable has put on the imperishable,
and this mortal has put on immortality,
then the saying that is written will happen,
"Death is swallowed up in victory."*

I Corinthians 15:54

These bodies of the embodied Self,
who is eternal, indestructible and unknowable,
are said to have an end.
Therefore fight, Arjuna.

II:18

*They shall perish but you shall endure;
yea, all of them shall wear out like a garment.
As clothing you shall change them,
and they will change,
but you are the same,
and your years shall have no end.*

Psalm 102:26,27

*Let everyone abide in the same calling
in which they were called.*

I Corinthians 7:20

The Self is not born, nor does it ever die;
having been, it will never cease to be.
Unborn, eternal, unchangeable and primeval,
it is not slain when the body is slain.

II:20

*We know that if our earthly tent were dissolved,
we have a building of God,
a house not made with hands,
eternal in the heavens.*

II Corinthians 5:1

❖

Whoso knows the Self as indestructible,
eternal, unborn and imperishable—
whom do they slay or cause to slay,
and how, Arjuna?

II:21

*Have the gates of death been opened to you,
or have you seen the doors of the shadow of death?*

Job 38:17

Just as one casts off worn out clothes
and puts on new ones,
even so the embodied Self casts off worn out bodies,
and enters other new ones.

II:22

*The Lord kills and makes alive;
he brings down to the grave and brings up.*

I Samuel 2:6

If you think of the Self
as always being born and always dying,
even then, Arjuna, you should not grieve.

II:26

I, even I, am he that comforts you.
Who are you, that you should be afraid
of a man who will die and of the son of man,
who will become like grass?

Isaiah 51:12

Those, who eat the elixir of the sacrificial remains,
go to the eternal God.
This world is not for one without sacrifice,
much less the next world, Arjuna.

IV:31

Unless you eat the flesh of the Son of man
and drink his blood,
you have no life in you.
Whoever eats my flesh and drinks my blood
has eternal life,
and I will raise him up on the last day.

John 6:53,54

Whoever leaves the body,
thinking of Me alone at the time of death,
reaches My being.
There is no doubt in this.

VIII:5

"Lord, remember me
when you come into your kingdom."
Jesus said, "Truly I say to you,
today you shall be with me in paradise."

Luke 23:42,43

❖

Coming to Me, these high-souled ones
do not attain rebirth,
the ephemeral place of pain;
they reach Supreme perfection.

VIII:15

Just as sin has reigned to death,
so also grace may reign
through righteousness to eternal life
by Jesus Christ our Lord.

Romans 5:21

All worlds are subject to rebirth, Arjuna,
from the world of the creator, Brahma, and downward,
but in reaching Me,
there is no rebirth.

VIII:16

Whoever lives and believes in me
shall never die.
Do you believe this?

John 11:26

Transcending nature's three qualities,
which are the source of the body,
the embodied soul is freed
from birth, death, old age and pain,
and it attains immortality.

XIV:20

The creation itself shall be delivered
from the bondage to decay
into the glorious liberty
of the children of God.

Romans 8:21

This unmanifested, spoken of as the Imperishable,
is said to be the highest goal,
which having reached, none return.
That is My supreme abode.

VIII:21

I press toward the mark for the prize
of the high calling of God in Christ Jesus.

Philippians 3:14

I give eternal life to them,
and they shall never perish,
nor shall anyone take them out of my hand.

John 10:28

Whatever good result is declared to come
from the scriptures, sacrifices, austerities and gifts;
by knowing this, the yogi transcends,
and attains the supreme primeval Abode.

VIII:28

Therefore, leaving the principles
of the doctrine of Christ,
let us go on into perfection.

Hebrews 6:1

Soon he becomes righteous
and finds eternal peace.
Arjuna, know that My devotee never perishes.

IX:31

Now being freed from sin,
and becoming servants to God,
you have your fruit in holiness,
and the end is everlasting life.

Romans 6:22

Then the goal should be searched
from which having gone, none return again,
thinking, "I seek refuge in that primal spirit,"
from which streams forth the eternal activity.

XV:4

One who sows to the Spirit,
shall reap life everlasting from the Spirit.

Galatians 6:8

The sun, nor the moon,
nor fire illumines My Supreme Abode,
to which having gone, none return.

XV:6

The sun shall no longer be your light by day,
nor for brightness
shall the moon give light to you,
but the Lord shall be an everlasting light to you,
and your God shall be your glory.

Isaiah 60:19

❖

There are two entities in the world—
the perishable and the imperishable;
the perishable is all beings;
the unchanging is called the imperishable.

XV:16

As we have borne the image of the earthy,
we also shall bear the image of the heavenly.

I Corinthians 15:49

Whosoever hears it (the *Bhagavad Gītā*),
full of faith and finding no fault,
shall be released,
and attain the happy worlds of the righteous.

XVIII:71

Truly, I say, "One who hears my word
and believes in him that sent me
has everlasting life and shall not be condemned,
but is passed from death into life."

John 5:24

Performing all actions,
taking refuge in Me;
by My grace,
he reaches the eternal indestructible abode.

XVIII:56

Comfort your hearts,
and establish yourself
in every good word and work.

II Thessalonians 2:17

Keep yourselves in the love of God,
looking for the mercy of our Lord Jesus Christ
to eternal life.

Jude 21

Introduction to Notes

The comparisons made in *The Bhagavad Gītā and the Bible: Pearls of the Same Strand* are easier to grasp with a basic understanding of the following concepts. The Self, like the soul, is God immanent. God and Brahman are names for God transcendent. Krishna and Jesus Christ, incarnations of God to different parts of the world, represent the same universal God. Spirit is identical in essence although the name changes from Self, Krishna, Christ, Brahman and God. Therefore in this comparative book, the different names for Spirit are deemed equal and comparable.

The purpose of the Notes is threefold. First, the corresponding parallels are condensed to a form that reveals more clearly their interconnection. Second, when there is more than one comparable *Bible* parallel to the *Gītā* stanza, each parallel is matched to the particular part of the *Gītā* stanza to which it relates. Third, there is brief commentary to explain occasional parallels and their paraphrases. The *Gītā* stanzas are indicated by Roman numerals and the *Bible* passages are written in italics. Some of the obvious matching parallels are not presented in the Notes. Occasionally, part of a parallel is included only to define the personal pronoun. The parallels between the *Gītā* and Bible are separated by a colon or dash. Partial and complete parallels are designated by quotation marks. When the speaker's voice is uncertain, the personal pronoun found in *Bible* passages is identified with parenthesis. The personal pronoun in the *Gītā*, which is always capitalized and speaks with spiritual authority, is Krishna. The personal pronoun identifying the disciple in the *Gītā* is Arjuna. The devotee's voice in the *Bible* represents Paul, David and Job among others.

Notes

Work

II:41 "one thought of a resolute nature": John 14:6

II:48 "steadfast in devotion" and "Evenness is called yoga."—I Corinthians 13:7
Yogas are different methods that unite the seeker with God. Union with God brings about "evenness" of heart and mind.
yogi: one who practices yoga

IV:18 "My Father (God) works up to this time and I (Jesus Christ) work."

III:8 "perform your proper action": Romans 12:11
"the maintenance of the body is impossible for you without action": "an idle soul shall suffer hunger"

III:9 "This world is bound by action unless performed for the purpose of sacrifice."—Psalm 127:1

III:19 "perform the action which is your duty": "he who does the will of God"
"reaches the Supreme": "abides forever"'

III:22 "I have nothing to achieve in the three worlds (earth, heaven and nether), yet I engage in action": "there is no end of all his (God's) labor, nor is his eye satisfied with riches"

III:31 "freed from actions": "I will walk at liberty"

IV:14 "nor do I desire the fruit of actions": "ceased from his own works"
"not bound by actions": "entered into his own rest"
"Rest" or peace comes when one is not "bound" to the results of one's actions.

IV:20 "abandoning attachment to the fruit of action": "in whatever state I am, to be content with that"
"he does nothing at all, even when engaged in action": "I can do everything through Christ, which strengthens me." These parallels depict the unselfish work of karma yoga, where the ego is uninterested in the results from one's actions.

IV:23 "acts for the sake of sacrifice": John 6:38

XVIII:11 "it is not possible for embodied beings to abandon actions completely": Psalm 104:23
"he who abandons the fruit of actions": Psalm 37:23

XVIII:23 "action performed by one who does not desire the fruit": "you (God) establish the work of our hands upon us"
The desire for God to "establish the work of our hands" implies non-attachment to the results of one's actions.

XVIII:24 "one seeking to obtain desires": Ecclesiastes 2:10
"action which is performed with great effort": Proverbs 15:27

XVIII:6 "relinquishing attachment to the fruits": James 1:7

XVIII:48 "one should not give up the action one is born into": I Corinthians 7:20
"all undertakings are surrounded with defects": "That which is crooked cannot be made straight, and that which is lacking cannot be numbered."

XVIII:3 "some thoughtful ones declare that action should be abandoned as being evil": Ecclesiastes 1:3
"acts of sacrifice, giving and austerity should not be given up": "offer the sacrifices of righteousness"

V:12 "abandoning the fruit of action": "work of righteousness"
"The unsteady one, attached to the fruit through desire, is firmly bound."—"everything is full of labor"

XVIII:5 "acts of sacrifice, giving and austerity should be performed, not abandoned": Titus 3:8
"sacrifice, giving and austerity are the purifiers of the wise": "purify to himself (Jesus Christ) his own people, zealous of good works"
"sacrifice, giving and austerity" parallels "good works"

Discrimination

II:51 "abandon the fruit of action": "do not store for yourselves treasures upon earth"
"they go to the place free of evil": "where moth nor rust corrupts, and where thieves do not break through and steal"

II:52 "your mind transcends the mire of delusion": "when the perfect (love) comes"
"you will be disgusted at what has been heard": "that which is in part shall be done away with"
Data gathered through the sense organs, such as hearing, is always partial.

III:17 "satisfied in the Self, content only in the Self": "I shall be satisfied when I awake with your (God's) likeness."
Self is God indwelling in the body.

IV:36 "you shall truly cross over all sin": "iniquity is purged"
"by truth": "by the raft of wisdom"

IV:38 "finds this (wisdom) in time within the Self": "we will be like him (Christ)"
"wisdom" parallels becoming like Christ/Self

XVI:22 "reaches the Supreme Goal": "shall have the light of life"

V:16 "ignorance is destroyed by the wisdom of the Self": The light shining "out of darkness, has shined in our hearts, to give the light of knowledge of God's glory."
"ignorance" parallels "darkness"

V:23 "whoever can endure here on earth, the impulse arising from desire and anger, is happy": "count it all joy when you fall into diverse temptations"

"is disciplined": "knowing that the testing of your faith leads to patience"

VI:26 "bring it (the mind) under control of the Self": "bringing every thought into captivity to the obedience of Christ"
The Self is the indwelling Christ.

VII:14 "My divine illusion is difficult to transcend": "broad is the way that leads to destruction"
The divine illusion is the world of form, which always changes and ends in destruction.

"Those who seek Me only, cross over this illusion.—"he (God) shall pluck my feet out of the net"

IX:2 "immediately comprehensible, easy to perform": "For my (Christ's) yoke is easy and my burden is light."

"unopposed to righteousness": Psalm 85:13

"imperishable": Psalm 117:2

X:10 "I give the yoga (discipline) of discrimination": "I will give them a heart to know me (God)"

X:17 "In what aspects are You to be thought of by me, Lord?"—Psalm 19:14

XIII:11 "constancy in knowledge of the Self": "seek his (God's) face continually"

"seeing into the end of the knowledge of truth": "now we see face to face" and "then I shall know, even as I am known"
"I shall know God as God knows me" describes "then I shall know, even as I am known."

"ignorance": "we see through a mirror, darkly"

XIII:17 "the light of lights, that is said to be beyond darkness": "That God is light, and there is no darkness in him at all."

"it (the light) is knowledge, the object of knowledge": II Corinthians 4:6

"seated in the hearts of everyone": "has shined in our hearts"

XV:10 "the deluded do not perceive Him": "the material man does not receive the things of the Spirit of God"

"they see (the Lord), who possess the eye of knowledge": "they (the things of the Spirit of God) are spiritually discerned"

XV:11 "those of untrained self, the unintelligent, do not perceive Him": The world cannot receive the Spirit of truth "because it does not see him nor knows him."

"those striving yogis perceive Him dwelling in the Self": "you know him (the Spirit of truth) for he dwells with you and shall be in you"

XVI:24 "the scripture is your authority in deciding what should be done and what is not to be done": II Timothy 3:16

XVIII:57 "resigning by thought all actions to Me": Colossians 3:23

"resorting to the yoga of discrimination, think of Me always": Proverbs 23:26

XVIII:73 "I will do your word."—Psalm 119:30

VII:18 "for steadfast in mind, he resorts to Me as the highest goal": Proverbs 8:34

XVIII:20 "one indestructible being in all beings": "so we, being many, are one body in Christ"

XVIII:21 "that which sees separation": "there is envying, strife and divisions among you"

XVIII:22 "that which clings to one thing as if it were all": Proverbs 26:16

XI:8 "with these eyes of yours": "the spirit of the world"
"I give you a divine eye": "the spirit which comes from God"
The "divine eye" implies spiritual sight.
"behold My majestic Yoga": "that we may know the things God has freely given us"

Devotion

VII:30 "they, who know Me in the perishable existence": "Christ shall be exalted in my body"
The "body" pertains to "perishable existence."

VIII:14 "when he constantly thinks of Me": "if we hold the beginning of our confidence steadfast until the end"
"I am easily reached": "we become partners of Christ"

IX:14 "always glorifying Me": "Lord, I have loved the dwelling of your house"
"reverent": "in the congregations I will bless the Lord"
"always steadfast", "striving with firm vows": "my foot stands in an even place"

IX:30 "even if the most evil worships Me, he is considered righteous": "if anyone is in Christ, he is a new being; old things have passed away"

XI:34 "by undistracted devotion alone can I be known of this form": I Corinthians 2:9

IX:22 "those who worship Me alone": "first seek the kingdom of God"
"I bring full security."—"all these things (food, water, clothing) shall be added to you"

XII:6,7 "those who worship Me": "because he has set his love upon me (God)"
"regarding Me as Supreme": "because he has known my (God's) name"
" I am soon the deliverer from the ocean of death and rebirth": "I will deliver him" and "I will set him on high"

XII:20 "those who follow this immortal law": "one who has and keeps my (Jesus Christ's) commandments"
"devoted": "loves me"
"they are very dear to Me": "I (Christ) will love and show myself to him"

XIII:10 "unwavering devotion to Me": Psalm 73:25
"retreating to solitary places": Isaiah 32:18
"aversion for wordly society": II Corinthians 6:14

XIII:25 "worship by hearing from others": "everyone who has heard and learned of the Father"
"they also transcend death, devoted to what they heard": "one who believes in me (Jesus Christ) has everlasting life"

XIV:26 "whoever serves Me with the unwavering yoga of devotion": "truly, my soul waits upon God"
"to become like God": II Corinthians 3:18

XVIII:67 —"do not give what is holy to the dogs, nor cast your pearls before swine"

XVIII:68 "having shown the highest devotion to Me, shall doubtlessly come to Me": "truly our fellowship is with the Father and with his Son"

VI:28 " always keeping the self steadfast": "we have trusted in his holy name"
"freed from sins": "that can present you as faultless"
"the yogi easily attains the infinite joy of contact with God": "to him (God) that is able to present you as faultless in the presence of his glory with exceeding joy"

IX:33 "reaching this transient and joyless world": "a dry and thirsty land where no water is"
"devote yourself to Me": "my soul thirsts for you (God)" and "my flesh longs for you (God)"

Renunciation

II:58 "when he completely withdraws the senses from the objects of the senses": "while we do not look at the things which are seen"
"his knowledge is steady": we look "at what is unseen (the eternal)"
Looking "at what is unseen" brings steadiness of knowledge because of the changeless quality of the formless.

II:59 "sense objects fade away from the fasting embodied one": "looking with diligence, so not to miss the grace of God"
Renunciation of sense objects establishes the spiritual sight that enables one to appreciate the grace of God.
"the taste" for "sense-objects": "no root of bitterness springs up to trouble you"
The "taste" for sense objects parallels "root of bitterness."
"on seeing the Supreme": "the kingdom of heaven is like a treasure buried in a field, which a man found"
The "Supreme" equals the "kingdom of heaven."
"his taste (for objects) ceases also": "Then from his joy, he sold everything and bought that field (the kingdom of heaven)."

IV:10 "freed from passion, fear and anger, absorbed in Me, purified by the austerity of wisdom": "the pure in heart"
"many have reached My being": "they shall see God"

V:25 “attain absorption in God”: “born of God”
“whose sins have been destroyed”: “they cannot sin”
“intent on the welfare of all beings”: “love their brother”

VI:2 “what they call renunciation”: “Set your affection on things above, not on things on the earth.”
“renounced self-interest”: “For you are dead, and your life is hid with Christ in God.”
Death in this passage speaks figuratively of renunciation of self-interest.

VI:4 “not attached to sense objects or to actions, renouncing all self-interest”: “what things were gain to me, those I counted loss”
“attained Yoga”: “for Christ” (union with Christ)
The attainment of yoga parallels union with Christ.

VI:24 “abandoning without exception all desires born of the will”: “denying ungodliness and worldly desires”
“completely restraining the senses”: “we should live soberly, righteously and godly in this present world”

XII:16 “indifferent, pure, disinterested, untroubled”: “for whose (Jesus Christ) sake I have lost everything and do count it as rubbish, so that I may win Christ”
“renouncing all undertakings and devoted to Me”: “I count everything a loss compared with the excellency of the knowledge of Christ Jesus”

XIII:8 “dispassion for sense objects”: “Do not love the world, nor the things that are in the world.”
“absence of egotism”: Proverbs 15:33
“insight into the evil of birth, death, old age, sickness”: Psalm 144:4
“insight into the evil of pain”: Romans 8:22

XV:5 "always dwelling in the Self," "the undeluded reach the Eternal goal": "stand fast in the liberty by which Christ has made us free"
"free from pride and delusion, with the evil of attachment conquered, rid of desires, released from the dualities": "do not be entangled again with the yoke of bondage"

XVIII:52 "dwelling in solitude": Psalm 102:6,7
"eating but little, subduing speech, body and mind": Philippians 4:5
"always engaged in the yoga of meditation": "I watch and am like a sparrow alone upon the house top" and Psalm 130:6
"cultivating dispassion": Proverbs 17:1

VI:10 "remaining in solitude, alone, with the mind and body controlled": Lamentations 3:28
"free from desire and possessions": I Timothy 6:8

XVIII:53 "abandoning egotism, force, pride, desire, anger, possessiveness; selfless and peaceful": "whoever will lose his life for my (Christ's) sake"
"one is fit to be one with God": Philippians 2:5,6

IV:21 "free from desire, with the mind and the self controlled": Luke 9:23
"relinquishing all possessions": Matthew 8:20
"doing bodily action only, he incurs no evil": Romans 6:7

Worship

IV:11 "by whatever way they approach Me, so I do reward them": Job 34:11
"people follow My path in every way": Proverbs 16:9

IV:25 "some yogis offer sacrifices to the gods": "whole burnt offerings and sacrifices"
"others offer themselves as a sacrifice": "to love him (God) with all the heart"

VI:31 "who worships Me as abiding in all beings": "to us there is only one God, from whom all things come"

VI:45 "who strives with diligence": "who hunger and thirst after righteousness"
"purified from sin": "pure in heart"
"reaches the supreme goal": "they shall see God"

XVII:28—"without faith it is impossible to please God"

IX:23 "those who worship other gods, also worship Me, though contrary to rules": "You shall have no other gods before me."

XI:44 "bowing down, prostrating my body, I ask you, adorable Lord, to forgive": Psalm 130:44

XII:5 "greater is their difficulty, whose thoughts are fixed on the Unmanifest": Ecclesiastes 7:34
"Unmanifest": "that which is far off and exceedingly deep"

VII:28 "those of pure actions, whose sin has come to an end, who are freed from the delusion of duality": "love out of a pure heart, a good conscience"
A pure heart can see the unity of spirit behind the seeming duality of the world.
"worship Me with firm resolve": "genuine faith"

XVII:11 "those desiring no reward, with a firm resolve in the mind that they should merely sacrifice": John 4:34
"in observation of the scriptures": Psalm 119:5

XVII:12 "sacrifice which is offered with a view for reward": Habakkuk 1:16
"sacrifice which is offered with a view for ostentation": Matthew 23:5

IX:13 "worship Me with mind turned to no other": I Samuel 2:2
"knowing Me as the imperishable source of beings": Lamentations 5:19

XVIII:36 "brings an end to pain": Revelation 21:4

Peace

II:65 "in peace all sorrows end": John 14:27
"the reason of the tranquil-minded soon becomes steady": Philippians 4:7

II:70 "when all desires enter, like waters enter the ocean, which becomes filled yet remains unaltered": "a handful of quietness"
"one who desires objects": "both hands full with trouble and vexation of spirit"

II:71 "the man finds peace": "I (Christ) will give you rest"
"who abandons all desires, acting without attachment, possessiveness": "come to me (Christ), all of you who labor and are heavily burdened"
"acting without egotism": "take my (Jesus Christ's) yoke upon you for I am meek and humble in heart"

IV:39 "Having attained wisdom, soon he reaches the supreme peace."—Proverbs 3:13,17

VI:15 "Always disciplining the mind, the yogi whose mind is subdued": "whose mind remains on you (God)"

VI:25 "One should withdraw little by little, with intelligence held in firmness." and "he should not think of anything": "be still"
"establishing the mind in the Self": "know that I am God"

XII:12 "abandonment": "you (God) also have performed all our works in us"

V:29 —"now acquaint yourself with him (God)"

Impartiality

V:15 "The omnipresent Lord does not take the evil or the good deed of anyone."—Job 35:6,7
"what do you do against him (God)?"
"wisdom is enveloped by ignorance": Isaiah 42:20

VI:9 "who is impartial": "It is not good to have respect of persons in judgment."

VI:29 "sees the same everywhere": "there is neither Jew nor Greek, slave nor free, male nor female"
"all beings in the Self": "you are all one in Christ Jesus"
The Self parallels the indwelling Christ.

VII:19 "the person of wisdom comes to Me": "having put on the new self, renewed in knowledge after the image of God that created him"
"realizing that Krishna is all": "Christ is all, and in all"

IX:29 "I am the same to all beings": Romans 2:11
"they who worship Me with devotion are in Me, and I am also in them": John 14:23

XIII:9 "non-attachment, absence of self-identification to son, wife, home and the like": Luke 14:26
"constant equanimity toward desirable and undesirable events": "godliness with contentment"

V:18 "to be absent from the body" and "We walk by faith, not by sight."—"the wise see the same"

Desire

II:14 "endure them (contacts with matter)": "Do not love the world, nor the things that are in the world."
"they (contacts with matter) come and go and are impermanent": "the world passes away"

II:62 "from attachment arises desire": James 1:14
"from desire arises anger": James 4:1

II:66 "to the unmeditative there is no peace": "the wandering of desire; this is also vanity and vexation of spirit"

III:34 "attraction and hatred are rooted in the object of each sense": "friendship with the world"
"attraction" parallels "friendship"
"The object of each sense" parallels "the world" because the world is made up of sense objects.
"one should not come under the sway of these two (attraction and hatred)": "do you not know that friendship with the world is enmity with God?"

III:36 "dragged on by what, does one commit sin": "the evil which I do not want, that I do"

III:37 "all devouring": "brings forth death"

III:38 "wisdom covered": Job 28:20,21
"wisdom covered by desire": Proverbs 18:1

V:22 "those delights born of external contacts": "there is a way which seems right to a person"
"those delights are truly sources of pain": "the end of that joy is heaviness"

VII:20 "they resort to other gods": I Corinthians 12:2

XIV:7 "the source of desire and attachment": "the eye is not satisfied with seeing, nor the ear filled from hearing"
"attachment to action": "all things are full of labor"

XVI:12 "given over to lust": "You have lived on earth in pleasure and self-indulgence."
"they seek hoards of wealth by unjust ways": "your riches are corrupted"

XVI:16 "entangled in the snare of delusion, addicted to the gratification of lust": "fall into temptation, a trap and into many foolish and hurtful lusts"
"they fall into a foul hell": "fall into temptation, which drown men in destruction and ruin"

XVI:21 "Therefore one should renounce these three."—
"lust": I Peter 2:11
"anger": Psalm 37:8,9
"greed": Proverbs 23:4

XVI:23 "whoso acts under the impulse of desire": "impure, covetous person, who is an idolater"
The desires of this world are idols.
"does not attain perfection, nor the Supreme Goal": "has any (no) inheritance in the kingdom of Christ and God"

XVI:8 "the universe is without a God": "The fool has said in his heart, there is no God."
"the universe is without truth, brought about by lust": Romans 1:24,25

XVI:11 "obsessed with immeasurable cares": "you who dwell upon many waters, abundant in treasures"
"ending only with death": "your end has come"

XVI:15 "I am rich and well born": "the rich man's wealth is his strong city"
"Who else is equal to me?"—"his own conceit"

Divine Manifestations

II:29 "no one understands the Self at all": "his (Lord's) greatness is unsearchable"
Self is the indwelling Lord.

IV:6 "I am birthless": "In the beginning was the Word, and the Word was God."
"the Lord of all beings": "everything was made by him"
"I am born by My own wondrous power." — "the Word (God) became flesh and lived among us"

VII:24 "the foolish ones regard Me, the unmanifest, as coming into manifestation": "you know me (Jesus Christ) and you know where I am from (Nazareth)"
"not knowing My higher, imperishable, unsurpassed nature": "he (God) that sent me (Christ) is real, whom you do not know" and Ephesians 4:10

VII:25 "I am not manifest to all, veiled by My mysterious power." and "this deluded world does not know Me": "The light shined in darkness, and the darkness did not comprehend it."

VIII:18 "the manifest proceeds from the unmanifest": Genesis 1:1,2
"all is dissolved in the unmanifest again": II Peter 3:10

IX:11 "the foolish disregard Me, who have taken a human form": "Who is a liar, if it is not he who denies that Jesus is the Christ?"
"not knowing My higher nature as the great Lord of beings": "who denies the Father (God)"

X:15 "You know Yourself through the Self": "I and my Father are one."

X:19 "My chief heavenly glories": "his (God's) work is honorable and glorious"
"there is no limit to My extent": Job 9:10

X:39 "I am also the seed of all beings": I Corinthians 15:38
"there is nothing, animate or inanimate, that can exist without Me": Acts 17:25

X:40 "there is no end of My heavenly glories": Job 5:9
"What I have described are only examples of My attributes."—Job 26:14

XI:41,42 "whatever was rashly said by me through carelessness" and "If in jest I insulted You at play, at rest, while sitting or eating": Luke 7:34

VII:5 "this (world) is My lower nature": "the first self is of the earth, earthy"
"distinct from this is My higher nature, in the form of indwelling souls": "the second self is the Lord from heaven"
"indwelling souls" parallels "Lord from heaven"

XIII:22 "spectator": Job 34:11
"permitter": Proverbs 16:4
"supporter": Isaiah 46:4
"enjoyer": Revelation 4:11
"the Great Lord": Psalm 147: 5
"the Supreme Self and the Supreme Spirit in this body": I John 4:13

XIII:29 "who sees all actions performed by material nature alone": "your way is in the sea, your path in the great waters"
"the Self not acting": "your (God's) footsteps are not known"

XIII:33 "so does the embodied Self illumine all bodies": "that (Christ) was the true Light which lights everyone"
"the great God is my womb": Job 31:15
"from that is the origin of all beings": Malachi 2:10

XV:9 "presiding over the ears, the eyes": "he (God) that planted the ear" and "he that formed the eye"
"He enjoys the sense objects."—"does he (God) not hear?" and "does he (God) not see?"

Omnipresence

VII:7 "there is nothing higher than I": "one God and Father of all, who is above all"
"All this is strung on Me as clusters of pearls on a strand."—"one God and Father of all, who is through all"

X:20 "I am the Self, seated in the heart of all beings": "I (Jesus Christ) am in my Father, you in me and I in you"

XI:13 "established in one, in the body of the God of gods": "are one body in Christ"
"with many divisions": "so we, being many"

XI:20 The "three worlds" refers to heaven, earth and the nether world.

Immortality

II:12 "nor shall we ever cease to exist hereafter": "this mortal has put on immortality" and "Death is swallowed up in victory."

II:18 "these bodies of the embodied Self are said to have an end": "they shall perish, all of them shall wear out like a garment"
"the embodied Self, who is eternal, indestructible" —"you (God) are the same and your years shall have no end"
"Therefore fight, Arjuna."—"Let everyone abide in the same calling in which they were called."
Arjuna was called to be a warrior.

II:20 "it (the Self) is not slain when the body is slain": "if our earthly tent (the body) were dissolved, we have a building of God"

II:21 "whom do they slay or cause to slay?": Job 38:17

II:22 "the embodied Self casts off worn out bodies": "the Lord kills"
"the embodied Self enters new ones (bodies)": "the Lord makes alive"

II:26 "you should not grieve": "who are you, that you should be afraid"
"grieve" parallels "afraid"

IV:31 "Those, who eat the elixir of the sacrificial remains, go to the eternal God."—"whoever eats my (Jesus Christ's) flesh and drinks my blood has eternal life"

"The next world" refers to heaven.

VIII:5 "thinking of Me alone at the time of death": "Lord, remember me when you come into your kingdom." One of the men, being crucified with Jesus, was thinking of him as death approached.

"reaches My being": "today you shall be with me (Jesus Christ) in paradise"

VIII:15 "do not attain rebirth; they reach Supreme perfection": "grace may reign through righteousness to eternal life by Jesus Christ"

"rebirth, the ephemeral place of pain": "sin has reigned to death"

Rebirth and death are different sides of the same cycle related to the perishable existence.

VIII:16 "in reaching Me, there is no rebirth": "Whoever lives and believes in me (Jesus Christ) shall never die." Krishna and Christ are equal, both being incarnations of one universal God.

XIV:20 "the embodied soul is freed from birth, death, old age and pain": "the creation itself shall be delivered from the bondage to decay"

"attains immortality": "shall be delivered into the glorious liberty of the children of God"

"Immortality" parallels the "glorious liberty" from pyschological time, which is said to be, living in the eternal now.

VIII:21 "this unmanifested is said to be the highest goal": Philippians 3:14

"that unmanifested": "God"

"that unmanifested, which having reached, none return": "they shall never perish, nor shall anyone take them out of my (Christ's) hand"

Jesus is Christ manifest. Christ, the Spirit, is unmanifest.

VIII:28 "whatever good result is declared to come from the scriptures, sacrifices, austerities and gifts; by knowing this, the yogi transcends": "leaving the principles of the doctrine of Christ"

"attains the supreme primeval Abode": "let us go into perfection"

IX:31 "soon he becomes righteous": "now being freed from sin and becoming servants to God, you have your fruit in holiness"

"finds eternal peace" and "know that My devotee never perishes": "the end is everlasting life"

XV:4 "the goal should be searched from which having gone, none return again": Galatians 6:8

XV:6 "that place which is My Supreme Abode": "the Lord shall be an everlasting light to you, and your God shall be your glory"

XV:16 "the perishable": "we have borne the image of the earthy"

"the imperishable": "we also shall bear the image of the heavenly"

XVIII:71 "whosoever hears it (the *Bhagavad Gītā*), full of faith": "one who hears my (Jesus Christ's) word and believes in him that sent me"

"shall be released" : "has everlasting life" and "is passed from death to life"

XVIII:56 "performing all actions": "establish yourself in every good word and work"

"taking refuge in Me": "keep yourselves in the love of God"

"by My grace, he reaches the eternal indestructible abode": "looking for mercy of our Lord Jesus Christ to eternal life"